Nanos gigantum humeris insidentes[1]

Greetings, U.S. Attorney for the Middle District of Florida, A. Lee Bentley, III,

These words may very well not reach your eyes. But, if I did not write them, then they stand for nothing- nor do I.

Because 'time is of the essence, I have been able to use my unique circumstances and choices to stand between the Social Injustice armed with a sword and shield of truth.

However, I ask but one favor in return- to those of with respect to whom read these words- to take the necessary time and patience to disseminate & digest this information.

And, if this favor is honored, I -with my limited capabilities- promise to illuminate the truth as I have uncovered it in the past three

---

[1] "We stand on the shoulders of giants by discovering truth by building on previous discoveries"- Issac Newton 1676; "If I have seen further, it is by standing on the shoulders of giants".

years in its complete accuracy and authenticity.

THE SPHERE OF INFLUENCE

At Whittier Law School, our moto was in service of Justice and Enterprise, but when does the service of Enterprise override the concept of Justice completely.

I believe Social Justice has been almost completely extinguished at Whittier Law School by a sphere of influence used to weed out individuals based off acts of discrimination, bias, deceit, and so forth.

Further, I believe that there is a false dichotomy in our society that believes the blue collar worker -with respect to whom operates under any authority- does so under a sphere of influence. And, within that sphere of influence, those individuals take steps every day where they encroach on others rights or exercise that authority within its scope.

The falsehood lies where we convince ourselves that these individuals must have complete mental strength, where they ignore the very acts explained above because of the consequences of that behavioral problem.

Even where individuals are mentally capable of repelling these small and overwhelming requests (such as the small encroachments everyday over others rights or the exercise of mere authority), we as a society must have recognized the benefit by now, nay the need, for physiological and psychiatric help-support.

Where this plea for help is ignored and those with respect of which pursue these alternatives, such as the use of medicinal marijuana or prescription medicine, lead to a megalomania complex and inevitable acts of discrimination and bias.

INTRODUCTION

My name is Dale Donald McGinnis, and to begin, almost everyone in my family has had the pleasure, nay the opportunity, to serve this great country.

However, after devastating events in my childhood, I was let to discover how I could accomplish this task after what had occurred so many years ago.

Specifically, I was born an identical twin with completely crossed-eyes. As a consequence, I received a very early education where I learned to focus and adapt before I could assimilate with children my age.

As a result, I have been under constant scrutiny from other children and teachers. For instance, in the first grade, I was separated from my twin brother in school because of our refusal to interact with other children.

Before I could even identify myself without my twin, my father who suffered from a mental and/or physical impairment himself, abandoned my family leaving us all vulnerable.

My mother, desperate to replace the father figure in our lives, married a sick, manipulative, abusive, and controlling man from a place of vulnerability. This man- through complete tyranny and brainwashing techniques- terrorized my family and drug us clear across the country.

After several years, I and my mother devised a plan to escape. However, before our family was torn apart for good and as the plan unfolded, my sister was kidnapped.

With the help of our community, friends and family, god and our country, my mother was able to slowly but surely piece our lives together. She sought aid from the Government in all forms including Social Security.

She worked forty hours a week to supplement that aid, and attended Nursing college where she became a Nurse to take care of her family.

And, she taught us to always fight for what we believe in where we were capable of anything as long as our mind, body, and soul were in the right place.

Naturally, during this time, my twin brother and my older brother were left to fill the shoes of my father and for when my mother could not be there for us. As a consequence, my brothers and I were constantly singled out because of our need for aid, for our religious affinities at the time, for our quality of life where we were extremely poor, and for our mental and or physical impairments aggregating from several factors.

And, on top of that, I received extra scrutiny because of my own unique physical and or mental impairments stemming from those factors and others. Specifically, because we were taken out of the public education system, we had to test back into school.

There, I tested one grade below my correlated age. However, after counseling, the education system decided that I suffered from an inability to adapt socially with other kids. Therefore, I remained in the grade below despite my abilities.

With this in mind- fast forward- I was able to adapt and receive, my education and other help, where the tools and techniques necessary to continue my education were out of reach in the past. Specifically, my merit, athletic ability, and musical talent allowed me to receive a merit and athletic scholarship.

Incidentally, from this experience, I was able to learn how to mold, contour, and improve behavior stemming from my physical and or mental impairment using these tools and techniques.

Therefore, throughout my college education in Missouri at a Private education institution, I critiqued and refined my capabilities giving back when I could to the community.

Specifically, during my life in college, I worked for and volunteer my time with the YMCA and an after-school Autism program. There I was able to learn from a broad spectrum of techniques and tools used to contour and mold these individuals behavior.

I also volunteer my time, where I was in a unique situation, for two Natural Disasters where my mother's home was damaged in Joplin, MO and her insurance company dropped her (and) my brother in the Air Force assisted other citizens in Minot, ND.

Additionally, I mentored my half-brother, where he suffered from his own physical and or mental impairment and the consequences stemming from a life in the incarceration system. Unfortunately, I learned that my understanding, my knowledge, and ability to help others not depended upon my own abilities but complete and autonomous choice by that individual, where I was forced to turn my half-brother into the authorities for breaking the law anonymously.

However, where I had no resources or the abilities to defend my mother or prevent my half-brother's relapse, I was able to preserve their rights. Specifically, in college, it was my hope to follow in my mother's footsteps. I studied pre-medicine because I was convinced I could find a cure for HIV that my twin brother had contracted at a young age.

After learning more about myself –my capabilities and inabilities in college- I changed my major to Philosophy. My reasoning was that with my photographic memory, my highly sensitive ability, and social awareness –as a consequence of my nature- I could learn to defend those who were in similar positions where they cannot defend themselves as I could not in the past.

However, although I was able derive the power behind ideas like wisdom, truth, and justice, I also uncovered the forces behind the stifling of these very voices. After being accused of the same accusations throughout my entire life and learning to obtain the ability and capability to succinctly and concisely communicate to my people, I decided to turn my attention to these interest to find an answer.

I decided to continue my education in order to learn to fight for myself and others in my position. I taught myself how to take the LSAT exam and improved my score from a 130's to 150's in three attempts. However, these attempts were admits a continual strive to give back to my community, my faith, my country, and to survive.

I needed to learn how to tap into my capabilities and abilities if I were to learn how to fight these forces and the increasing social injustice. Therefore, I moved to California in search of others with respect of whom stood behind the very force I wished to protect- Diversity.

After being offered a career position from the YMCA in orange county, I turned won the offer, moved to LA, and started work for a social media company, a hotel company in Beverly Hills, and eventually ran my own

Technical assistance company. My reasoning was to learn how society communicated using technology with the hope it would illuminate some truth.

I was not sure where I fit when it came to this mission. I applied for an officer position with the Army and with the LAPD. I passed the United States Army physical, mental, and background checks, however, the LAPD declined my application, stating that I was immature. Where I was ready to fight and appeal the LAPD's decision, I recognized that perhaps there was an important distinction here.

Additionally, what I discovered from working in Los Angeles was bad business practices and acts of discrimination and bias. Therefore speaking with an Employment Law Attorney, I chose to pursue Law School & drop my claims to protect my reputation and integrity moving forward.

I did research and applied to law schools all over the country. I received several offers, but

WLS's offer was based entirely off Diversity & offered the most amount of money. After reading Professor Reich article on Justice Oliver Wendell Holes, I decided to fight through Law school with the help of Whittier.

Therefore, the summer before law school, I flew to Wichita Falls, Texas- where my brother was stationed at the Air Force base with his wife- and worked to prepare for law school. There, I learned to deal with my procrastination and perfection complex. I wrote a book to focus and hone my skills- my purpose. I preserved my financial, criminal, and civil record where I applied for financial assistance from the Government.

I. THE WHITTIER LAW SCHOOL FAMILY

Whittier Law School wanted us to believe that we were a family. But, from my experience as explained supra, a family does not manipulate, control, deceive, and hurt the ones that they love.

The following is a discussion of those events where a highly sensitive individual who questioned everything, used vague language to avoid their dragnets, made the causal links leadings to the exposure of the sphere of influence, and maintained full disclosure and complete transparency.

This analysis is as separate form emotion – as individual can be- where the evidence is preserved through a discovery technique only compromised by private investigators and other discovery employed to slander and defame myself and others to envelop this behavior over time.

As a man of consistency, a man who likes to make things simple by attempting to put them in the strongest form of our memory- a picture. Therefore, I present this consistency and the imagery so that I may provide the clearest of picture.

It is a precept that the following discussion of the events that occurred over the last three years of my Law School education hinges on choice.

Because, where I choose to attend Whittier Law School based upon Diversity, my choices to constantly shape that education were eliminated and stifled by the following acts of discrimination, deceit, bias, manipulation, and fraud.

Additionally, as explained briefly supra, it is my goal to present a clean and unambiguous picture using evidence of a methods, a scheme, process, and common plan of those acts.

The following is a detailed narrative of these events:

I. A SPHERE OF INFLUENCE: OVER INTERNSIPS, ALUMNI, AND ADMINISTRATION

To begin, I shall start with my first reported act(s) of discrimination, where the initial report to the ABA was not filed (a pattern of neglect to report that will be enveloped as well infra).

I applied for a Volunteer Internship with Ziptax (a tax fire, i.e. Mytax) during the summer of my second year at Whittier Law School. I met with the supervising attorney Joseph Ursic where in our interview we shared our experiences at Whittier Law School with Professor Rosenblatt (director of Intellectual Property Fellowship and certification) and my intentions of taking Federal Income Taxation with Professor Manasfi.

Initially, I applied for an externship, as the program would provide the building block for Federal Income Taxation, an area I had decided to pursue professionally after the events that occurred (as explained supra).

However, I accepted the Volunteer internship where I explicitly stated that my financial ability rested on federal loans. Therefore, I could only afford to work for as long as I cold afford to travel and so forth.

There, I learned of the opportunity from Professor Manasfi & WLS, as they approved and sponsored the program. Additionally, my two supervising attorneys were alumni of WLS.

Unfortunately, and repeatedly shown over time, I discovered substantial insufficiencies with the program. Specifically, the supervising attorneys did not have enough work for the number of interns, they neglected to communicate where they did not know our names, and several other insufficiencies.

And, when my financial abilities became insufficient, I asked to continue my work from home. I stated that because of the lack of supervision and work; working from home would benefit both parties. However, after my attendance and abilities were slandered and after being called out by an associate for a mistake out of my control, both supervising attorney's stated my tenure was effective immediately.

Then, I was threatened with additional charges and fines, and my reputation was damaged with my associates and Whittier Law School, where my supervising attorney alerted the director of professional and career services. Additionally, although I was unaware of the sexual orientation of my supervising attorneys, they had made comments and statements of which I could derive they did not know my name; were possible homosexual themselves; possibly did not know I was homosexual; and did not know of my physical and or mental impairment.

Following these events, I informed Joseph Ursic of my intent of reporting these substantial insufficiencies, as well as my belief I was the target of discrimination. Specifically, where I was being discriminated against for my financial ability, my sexual orientation, and my physical and or mental impairment.

Therefore, I wrote the director of professional and career services. As a result, the Director called me and requested to meet in person. As a further result, Joseph request to speak over the phone. However, both explained that the situation arose because of my inability to communicate properly, my attendances, and that I needed to learn how to maintain my relationships within the corporate structure.

The Director assured my that I was very luckily that the situation was resolved peacefully and would not effect me in my future endeavors. Further, Joseph Ursic over the phone stated that my reputation would not be in danger where they only report to others for job inquires.

I was unaware the Director did not file my report and that the experience would continue to effect my education moving forward.

II. A SPHERE OF INFLUENCE: OVER PROFESSORS

Unfortunately, these acts were the start and the furtherance of on-going discriminatory acts. Continuing on, I enrolled in Federal

Income Taxation my third year fall semester at Whittier Law School. With all intentions of putting the past behind me, I discovered the same substantial insufficiencies stemming from Professor Manasfi.

Here, Professor Manasfi failed to attend several classes, failed to schedule make-up classes within the class schedule, respond to requests to meet in person, respond to correspondence and telephone calls upon request, and release a final review and material on an equal footing to all students.

Therefore, when I flew to Texas to spend Thanksgiving with my family for the first time in three years, I was left unaware of make-up classes and a review session. Upon returning home for my final exams, I took the exam based off the limited information available from my text books, my internship, the incomplete PowerPoints available off twin, and what I had taught myself.

Additionally, I texted and called the only student I knew in the class- where she completely ignored me (a student who later who file a lawsuit against students and attempt to associate with me where she was friendly with Professor Manasfi).

In my mind at the time, the only reasoning behind such behavior from the professor, the students, and the timing was a comment I made to the professor the day I interviewed with SBA's NDRLC when on my way to class. There, I made a specific comment to her on my way to class stating that I had been with my partner for 2 ½ years. However, later I would find out that this information would lead to the tipping off and the cover up of these acts infra.

During the same semester, and on a related note, I took a course required by WLS called Lawyering Skills 4. A class taught by two individuals, Professor Berman and Professor Snider.
The next series of events starting two weeks into my last semester led to the beginning of an increased level of scrutiny by myself.
After completing all requires assignment

through an interactive online program Moodle, attending all classes, and taking the final – as was the same with federal income taxation- the following events took place:

Within this period, Professor Schnier announced she was leaving WLS to pursue an opportunity elsewhere, both Professor Manasfi and Professor Pritikin exercised their contract option to leave WLS at the end of the year, Whittier Law School announced an attempt to sale the land to Whittier College, our alumni stepped down and a new alumni was formed, the dean stepped down, and I was informed that I failed my federal income taxation final and Lawyer skills 4.

III. A METHOD, PROCESS, SCHEME, AND COMMON PATTERN OF A SPEHERE OF INFLUENCE: TO WEED OR NOT TO WEED

Therefore, I devised a plan to begin an investigation into the methods, scheme, process, and common plan where WLS, WC, and certain professor(s) (and or agents) took substantial steps to 'weed' out students based off discrimination and unacceptable business practices.

And, to collect this evidence that Whittier Law school, like an incident in 2011, would attempt to cover up these acts without taking responsibility using unacceptable business practices and or methods like grade manipulation.

a. DEFAMATORY STATEMENTS AND GRADE MANIPULATION BASED OFF DISCRIMINATION AND BIAS

To begin, having had collected and meticulously organized all my documents relating to my professional and educational development at Whittier Law School, I began looking, and this is what I discovered:

The first year of my law school education a defamatory comment by Professor Webster was published by a student (unbeknownst to me, considering I chose to opt out of social media application).

The same year, I was criticized openly in class in the same manner by Professor Welkowitz. This statement, although not published or written down, had the same effect. Following finals, my two lowest grades were coincidently from these professor(s), where I would take another course with Professor my second year where he lashed out again and gave me the same grade.

Upon protests of these grades to Assistant Dean of Student and Alumni Relations (Nidhi Parih Vogt), Professor Webster had already flown out of the country, where he called me and met with me only after we both returned from SummerAbroad.

There, in that meeting several moths later, he stated that I lacked a command of information and challenging my ability to recall the facts of his exam. After Professor Webster assured me that my grade was a reflection of my inabilities, the assistant dean of student and alumni relations assured me and discouraged me from protesting my grade. Additionally, I was informed by other students that other students were only able to improve their grades after submitting several pieces of work and learning from his constructive criticism, further discouragement.

However, after going through my documents, I had determined that Professor Webster only gave constructive criticism to students at random and for students who were able to meet with him in person. Those students, either transferred or did extremely well.

In fact, on the same note, this reminded me of the same argument I had with Professor Martin, my legal writing instructor, who asked what I wanted when protesting a grade. There, the concept I continually protested was that I only wanted to have the grade that was a reflection of my performance. There, she stated that I lacked the ability to apply these skills.

Upon losing my Diversity scholarship, considering the debt and my grades, I had to re-analyze my ability to pay for my education as well as my professional career in the future.

b. A SPHERE OF INFLUENCE CONTINUED: INTERNATIONAL INTELLECTUAL PROPERTY INTERNSHIP PROGRAM

Therefore, I applied for WLS's Summer Abroad and a newly founded international intellectual property internship program in China. It was my intention to use my aw degree as a foundation for my new found interest in entrepreneurship. Therefore, I submitted my resume, applied for a passport, and made financial plans to travel and stay in China for the summer.

However, without missing a step, I discovered substantial insufficiencies in both. Upon arriving in Shanghai, China and settling in, I took the subway to the firm. Unfortunately, my supervising attorney was unable to fulfill his role for various reasons where he had no knowledge of American law, was unable to communicate effectively in English, and had no program or tasks.

Therefore, Professor Mertus and the supervising attorney suggested we write a publishable article. However, we received no help editing, creating, or finishing these articles. Additionally, after asking advice from several professors as suggested, not one professor would comment or lend an ear. In fact, when corresponding directly to Professor Rosenblatt – head of intellectual property and a Harvard graduate- she would not respond at all. Further, upon running into her at an Intellectual Property event, she stated that she did not respond because I was 'too vague'.

Having read all of professor Rosenblatt's law review articles and speaking to her about them, I found this disturbing. At this point, I immediately wrote my friend who was given a coinciding internship in Beijing at another Law Firm. There, the firm had treated him entirely different where he was constantly engaged and given tasks as well as feedback and comments. Moving forward, my friend who worked at the same firm as I – where we decided to stay in touch- decided to transfer to Loyola.

The next step of the Summer Aboard program were classes & educational field trips in Beijing and Nanjing. However, again, I discovered substantial insufficiencies in the courses and the field trips.

    a. **A SPHERE OFINFLUENCE CONTINUED: SUMMERABROAD PROGRAM, EDUCATION FIELDTRIPS, AND THE ABA FAILURE TO REPORT AN ACT OF DISCIRMINATION**

Some of the field trips were to locations that had little to no educational value where they were primarily profit for those individuals and probably the professor. The classes, although primarily lecture, were small, the student would not comment, and most students would not or could not contribute.

With the exception for a few upperclassmen would respond, but without a clear control over the material, and as if, these particular students were under a sphere of influence. These students were particularly close to the professors.

There, I developed a theory, that possibly the professors and/or WLS were controlling the discussion and or the student's behavior. Specifically, at one of our only educational field trips, I was able to see this process unfold.

On the way to a Non-profit employment law firm, after listening to the aba auditor share her experience in African American heritage and conflict (her papers), I shared my experience in Belleville, Illinois.

There, I told her how odd it was for me in college to see a KKK rally in such a modern time. Following this comment, I explained that this was probably due to political, cultural, social, and economical factors in that particular area. Additionally, I explained the area of my studies when I lived in that area- Victimology.

After the brief discussion, Professor Mertus and Donni, as well as the students, spread the word of my conversation. Unaware of this nor that I or the ABA auditor could have been offended regarding our friendly conversation, a meeting was set-up the following morning though an email.

Because I was – at the time- writing on to Law school, I did not receive the email (or) did not read it. Because everyone showed up at the meeting besides me, my friends informed me that Professor Mertus stated that the only person this message needed to reach was not there (indicating that it was meant for me).

That message was to instruct us to be careful what we say around the AB instructor and that it would be best if we remain silent. This was exactly the method, process, scheme, and common pattern- where WLS & professors would attempt to prohibit and or control students voices.

Upon discover this meeting, the message, its recipient, and the speaker; I reported the act to the ABA instructor through skype (upon her request). There, after politely listening, she insisted that although this act was wrong- I did not have enough proof.

Therefore, after returning home, receiving my grades, and being accepted into law review, I decided to continue my education at Whittier Law School besides these inconsistencies.
My hope was to move beyond the acts- considering my grades and accomplishments. However, the thought never crossed my mind that these grades (or) my achievement was a cause of my report.

       c. **A SPHERE OF INLFUENCE OVER EXTRA CIRRICULAR ACITIVITES, THE STUDENTS,**

AND ALUMNI: GRADE MANIPULATION

Therefore, with the past acts of the Professor and Whittier law school, I moved forward with an open heart, but a keen-eye.

Upon scheduling for my second year fall semester at Whittier law school, the assistant dean of student relations, Dean Vogt, informed me that I had to enroll in legal methods because my GPA fell below 3.0.

Immediately I protested, stating that the effects of such a request would effect my choice to engage in area of my interest, because the class (although possibly beneficial) would take away (or) make my other obligations increasingly difficult and unable to accomplish (like law review).

There, she stated that I could appeal to take more courses, but that would most likely be denied based on my current performance and GPA. Additionally, that these courses would cost me additional funds, and that in fact, my appeal had been denied where no reasoning or formal response was given in return of the request for appeal.

That semester, My 2L Fall year, I discovered that in fact the discrimination acts were on-going where- because of incidents in the past- classmates, friends, professors, and associates where under the sphere of influence and being controlled by Whittier Law School.

However, there were exceptions to the control where individuals and professors would help assist, but with fear of retaliation in various forms.

That specific semester, and the following, every course ran by a professor under such control would issue the same grade along the same lines. In fact, they were the same grade as the two grades that were acts of discrimination my 1st year.

Without fail, each exam employed the same tactics in this grade manipulation. However, at this time, my findings were inconclusive without more. Therefore, after finishing my intellectual property certification and fellowship, I was able to switch my concentration to Business Law. Three, I was under the impression I could isolate the methods and process that WLS employed when manipulating grades.

   d. **A SPHERE OF INFLUENCE USED TO WEED OUT STUDENTS, NOT JUST BY GRADE MANIPULATION**

However, I also uncovered a thicker method, process, scheme, and common plan to "weed" out students. Upon request, the Assistant Dean and my current Professor of evidence, notified me that he wished to speak with me. After insisting he state the reason, I was told I was under investigation, and he would not disclose for what reason.

In that meeting, Professor Pritikin stated that he was of the belief I had broken the school's code against plagiarism and that I had broken some code of conduct. However, after having studied the school policy and code, I challenged him on these grounds. In fact, I pointed towards a form & process of my own that I had maintained all semester that conclusively rebutted his claims. Further, he then claimed that I had plagiarized my paper for Law review. Again, I explained that there may have been familiar language, but because of the closed universe and the purpose behind the write-on exam, his grounds were unfounded. I then presented him with my Law Review paper that I submitted to Law review reflect that same method process.

Continuing, he began to bring up incidents where I had appealed to the students in charge of Trial Ad where I protested that this club was unfairly recruiting members and preventing others students from enjoying or committing and helping the team.

After rebutting his claims that I was overly aggressive towards these students, he then began to bring up the previous incident in China. I immediately insisted that he tell me how he became aware of these facts, and he stated that Professor Mretus had told him.

I immediately disclosed all information upon his request, remained transparent, and protested that his investigation was unfair and put a substantial burden on me where this issue was in the past. After he received all the information, he stated that he would get into contact with me if he needed anything else. Additionally, he gave me the same grade that reflected the manipulation of grades my first and second year.

It was then that I made the causal connection between WLS method, process, scheme, and common plan to "weed" out students with grade manipulation and also extra circular activities at school, including our Moodle program.

e. **A SPHERE OF INFLUENCE WITH ALUMNI AND STUDENTS**

Therefore, I prepared to try out for as many of these programs as possible to uncover this Dragnet. It started with Moot Court, then Alternative Dispute Resolution, and finally UCLA'S 2016 Environmental Law Negotiation. Additionally, I held positions in two student organizations. Here, I found WLS using the exposure, other students and alumni, Moodle and the school policy, and each process to collect anything that would incriminate the students and weed them out.

For Moot Court, specifically, I employed the same writing process so that I would avoid the dragnet set via the policy code for plagiarism, but ran into bias and discrimination within the process (for example the selection of judges).

There, the alumni and various students heard my presentation and acted in furtherance of that discrimination. There, I was able to hear comments from a particular alumni (DA attorney had commented that I would be an excellent trial attorney and that my conception of justice was wrong). Upon receiving news of the result, I requested the comments and grading, but was told by Catherine and the school that these were not 'available'.

There, I uncovered a causal link between the Alumni, where they would place past students within our school programs to judge other students and throughout other process. Following, these alumni and students – under the sphere of influence- would be used in furtherance of WLS's goals of weeding out students and grooming others for certain favorable positions.

Such as -----, who I competed against in Moot Court, with respect to whom his brother was one of the officers that made comments with my arresting officers.

Specifically, like Moot Court, the competition judges at UCLA 2016 Environmental Competition were bias under this sphere of influence where they asked specific questions regarding my tone and how other students reacted to remarks, suggesting that I was overtly aggressive with no basis for such questions.

Additionally, Professor Reich insisted on taking picture with me where it was his goal to have this picture places on the front page of Whittier Law School's page, a part of the school's strategy. However, I did not protest this picture because I felt it was evidence of a particular behavior I would be unable to find a causal link. Therefore, this practice to collect transcripts, provoke students and obtain incriminating transcript and/or writing these comments to the BAR at extra curricular activities where the judges were apart of the sphere of influence, and publish pictures of the students receiving rewards and/or at events was all an attempt to cover up liability and a complete misuse of each individual's achievement and use of image.

f. A SPHERE OF INFUENCE WITH WHITTIER COLLEGE

Moving forward, and bringing us back full circle to my third year last semester and upon discovering this sphere of influence, my goal next was to investigate how far the sphere of influence went. To begin, I focused on my Federal Income Taxation.

My reasoning was that if I could isolate the process behind this particular act of manipulation it might lead me towards answers. Therefore, I researched cases unique to my circumstance finding a website[2]. There, I found that in 2011- in response to a request for deposition in regards to grade manipulation- Whittier law school had settled that case and released that employee.

Therefore, to build a case, I constructed declarations that would lead towards responses that would illuminate truth. Once I questioned my professor, I quickly discovered that her basis behind my grade was attendance. Attendance is considered at Whittier Law School in three ways where a student must protest to take an exam where attendance is at issue. She insisted we meet in

---

[2] http://whittiergate.com/aba.htm

person and discuss employment or other benefits and the exam.

Then upon further questioning, she resorted to relevancy and attached the assistant dean to the conversation instead of explaining her reasoning. Further, upon requesting to see my exam (and) examining her responses and grade to my answers, I found evidence of further discrimination and grade manipulation using a policy question.

Specifically, a policy question where I argued for the blue collar worker and against the path of law that I believed was leading to unfair advantages and manipulation within the area of tax law through legislation.

There, she manipulated grades specifically reducing my grade based off insufficient reasons on a specific policy question. And, when put on notice, the professor emailed faculty stating that we were going to review the exam to make further changes to the grade.

IV. STIFLING THE MINORITY AND THE DIVERSE: AN ON-GOING COVER UP OF A SPHERE OF INFLUENCE AND THE CHILLING EFFECT

At this point, I considered the steps WLS had taken as Fall Semester classes began, where they attempted to sale the land, changed the alumni association, had the current dean step down, allowed certain teachers to exercise their option contracts, and more.

There, at this point, it was that I discovered a causal link between the Alumni, the students, WLS, and WC- where the law school attempted to cover up their past, current, and future liability using Whittier college and the newly founded alumni using ambiguous language and unauthorized practices.

Additionally, WLS began to release the specific professor's that had open themselves open to liability as explain supra. Specifically, professor Pritikin, Manasfi, and others. Further, WLS released the Dir. Of

Career services and s0 forth. Therefore, upon finding these causal connections, I found that there were further steps taken.

a. DOMAOCLES' SWORD: INSTITUATIONALLY CREATED COURSES TARGETING STUDENTS

However, what I discovered was a plan to take substantial steps further to weed out students that had opened WLS, WC, alumni and others up to liability. Further steps were taken to collect incriminating evidence and so forth to slander theses students. The reasoning was to create a chilling effect and to substantial burden any individual who resisted the sphere of influence.

Therefore, upon manipulating grades, WLS created LS4(2) and put a sword over the heads of a particular set of students where they were forced to perform under BAR conditions or not graduate. After speaking with these students and discovering that they had subsume to the same treatments and even treatment substantially further then I had experience (at this point).

b. SOCRATES APOLOGY: USE OF PROFESSORS, STUDENTS, AND ALUMNI TO PROVOKE AND BEHAVE IN A WAY TO SUPPORT PAST ACTS- AN UNFAIR AND BIASED FACILITATION OF A DISCRIMINATION REPORT

Further, WLS continued the on-going discrimination and sphere of influence through professors. Specifically, in my Federal Courts with Professor Pathak, which leads to my second report of a violation of the non-discrimination policy.

There, I took substantial steps to reserve the rights of my students and I where the same behavior was being exhibited by the students and the professor (as explained supra). I reported the exact behavior from the students and the professor I had experience based off the sphere of influence.

Specifically, I reported a student stating that class agreed we should remain quite and not ask because the professor and the students wanted to be programmed so that they can learn what they needed to pass the BAR. This particular student was a friend of mine and would not a remark like this without a foundation. At this point, it did not occur to me that he could be under the same pressure as everyone else under the sphere of influence.

Upon reporting the students comment and the teachers repeated absences and lack of control, I explained my theory of how I was the victim of an act of on-going discrimination based of this sphere of influenced (explaining the situation in federal income taxation).

There, the Assistant Dean of student and alumni relations and the assistant dean Pritikin, claimed to represent an unbiased neutral group where they acted in the same manner and method as before. Where they requested to meet, asked for full disclosure and transparency, and attempted to convince me that my rights were no founded (and or) did not exists. An act that every single person under this sphere of influence would attempt.

After fighting for my rights, protesting the bias, and my right to appeal, WLS found no evidence of discrimination. Therefore, I devised a plan to give WLS a choice to resolve the liabilities I had uncovered, while at the same time making full disclosures with the OCR and maintaining transparency.

c. A SPHERE OF INFLUECE: WHITTIER COLLEGE UNFAIR AND BIAS APPEAL PROCESS

I was unaware that it may be possible the sphere of influence extended to the BAR and/or individuals within the OCR organization. My reasoning behind this method was that other students had came forward stating that they had been accosted by the same methods, manners, and scheme.

There, they had specifically identified instances where Moodle and other tactics were used to weed them out: such as letter to the BAR, DUI's. LS4(2), manipulation of grades, and more. Therefore, in my appeal, I used a memorandum addressing these liabilities with hope to resolve these issues.

Additionally, I crafted a poll of 50 neutral questions where the purpose was to derive other students WLS experience. I issued the poll out to every single student who held a position within the SBA. Because my theory was that the sphere of influence reached these students, I anticipated individuals would be extremely upset about protecting heir reputation and etc. where a small amount of students had experienced a chilling effect and more as explained supra.

Immediately after this poll was released, after WC requested to meet, requested full disclosure and transparency, WC closed the case stating that they had found no grounds for discrimination.

V. A SPHERE OF INFLUENCE THAT GOES TOO FAR: THE ABA, OCR, ADMINSTRATIVE EMAIL SYSTEM, DOCTORS, LAWYERS, POLICE OFFICERS, AND MORE

Following these events, WLS immediately made steps to cover up this liability with the students where I asked for assurances and protection. As a result, I was targeted.

There, I became the target of multiple private investigators, retaliation from teachers and students, and alumni through other channels where the sphere of influence had reached. These were the same substantial steps taken to stifle and prevent other students from being heard.

Therefore, in that time, I discovered the following tactics employed by W/C, WLS, students, friends, Private investigators, alumni, my lawyer, my doctors, and other individuals that would prevent me (or attempt to) form voicing my opinion and continuing my education and way of life in California.

First, WLS used Prof. Pathak where she mimicked Prof. Manasfi's acts in order to cover up or support her acts. There, I protested the behavior in its entirety and made an additional report of discrimination.

Professor Pathak was late to several classes like Professor Manasfi. She attempted to communicate strictly through TWEN (an online program). She attempted to direct the classes conversation into holding a make-up class outside of the class schedule. And, she directly pointed me out in front of the class- where I merely spoke from an objective standpoint. Additionally, there, another student acted out in a discriminatory during that incident- where she had a special relationship with the professor (specifically a job interviews with the DA).

Secondly, WLS took substantial steps to collect incriminating evidence against myself in the privacy of my home, the privacy my private school, the confidence I had in my friends and colleagues, and through the confidence instilled in mentors and individuals associated with the extra curricular activities.

In the privacy of my home, the first private investigator contacted me through a gay application after my partner and I of 2 ½ years went different directions. There, he took pictures of my I.D., videos of myself, asked incriminating questions, purchased items, and other acts all to the degree that I identified him as a spy.

The second private investigator, as well as the third, approached me in the privacy of my gym. I attended this gym for the past three years, as explained supra, for holistic reasons and to shape my behavior. There, one asked how one would hide the symptoms of drugs by exercising. The other indicated that, from his experience, being video taped is more showing then one normally admits. Where this conversation was in the context of an athletic event, it correlated directly with WLS's steps to video tape and record our classrooms, and my choice to pursue extra curricular activities where I would be put on a higher level scrutiny.

The fourth private investigator approached me in the only gay bar in my area. After speaking with the investigator, he explained that he was married, was not from this state as he was a traveling accountant, and that he met his husband on a plane randomly (showing me his ring). Additionally, he explained that his flight left in the morning, his phone was dead, and that he needed a ride home (asking repeatedly). Against my better judgment, I gave him a ride following his direction that he put into my phone. On the way, I was pulled over within minutes of departure. Following, I was lied to by police officers, not allowed to use the restroom, refused phone calls where my phone was not in service, abused where I refused to provide vitals, defamed and slandered and put into a cell for 12+ hours, and released on two charges of Driving While Under the influence.

Therefore, at school, based upon what they had gathered, that is, where they recorded a specific classroom, collected transcripts from competitions they knew I would be apart of influence individuals on the panel, used students and professors in attempts at confrontation, made several attempts to deceive me into signing the exit interview form and another form labeled 2015.

Additionally, they had professors make comments through legal analysis workshop.

I had hired an attorney and was seeing a doctor. Because at this point, I was afraid how far the sphere of influence went. After calling the data bank that held the records for the tests I requested from my doctor, I discovered my doctor had negligently failed to process a prostate test, leading to permanent damage to my prostate and ability to urinate and process liquids. Additionally, my doctor negligently failed to order the correct tests that reflected that I was not under any sort of influence whether it be drugs or abuse thereof. Where I insisted on checking my blood and urine for STD's, drugs, and other ailments, upon further discovery I found he had neglected to take my tests at all. And, repeatedly ordered the wrong tests and requests additional sample of urine that would disappear where I saw the arrest officer leave the parking lot in his patrol car 10 minutes before my appointment. An appointment that only the doctor, my school, and myself knew about.

After careful research, I hired an attorney that I thought would be free from this influence for my DUI. However, if he was not, then I knew I would not be safe in California nor would my rights be preserved or upheld in this sphere of influence.

My reasoning was that there was a causal connection between these patterns, methods, processes, and common schemes with WLS, WC, alumni, the students, and the particular network of individuals from Harvard- a sphere of influences. Considering prof. Pathak, pritkin, rosenblat, martin, and others that graduated from these schools. Therefore, I requested a conflict check and was assured that my attorney was not apart of this sphere of influence or a conflict.

After assuring me that he knew of no one, then he informed me that in fact he did know an individual alumnus from the district attorney. Accordingly, he continued to discouraged me from perusing the case and using my situation, his agreement to represent me, my inadequate understanding of the law, and the timing of the essence with the DUI to the same effect and behavior as the parties described above.

There, he stated that because of a meeting he had with the managing partner they were afraid of the liability that my case carried. Therefore, as a consequence, they would be performing their job without charging me but would not pursing the case from my philosophy.

Finally, and with great effort, I was able to isolate these issues, document them, finish my papers; presentations; assignments, and tests. However, I discovered that the Director of Financial Services was released private documents and released the exam numbers out to the administrative email system – to each individual student – where there was no reasonable notice and I had made specific protests that this email system was compromised.

There, the assistant dean, upon being notified by myself, stated that he was tired of me wasting the administrative time with my delusion fantasies. The same language that was used by prof. Pathak when I spoke to her in person, the arresting officers, professor manasfi, joseph ursic, students, alumni, and the private investigators. This causal link that I was perceiving events as they did not appear gave me the proof that I needed to reach the conclusion that the situation was out of OCR's ability (and) that my life was in danger.

VI. TO FIGHT ANOTHER DAY: ADMINSTRATIVE EMAIL SYSTEM AS AN UNAUTHORIZED BUSINESS PRACTICE AND AN INVASION OF PRIVACY

Therefore, I fled to Missouri where I stayed with my family at a substantial burden. I explained everything to my family, and I decided to write these words. I then flew to Florida to stay with my twin brother.

Since then, Whittier Law School has used its Administrative Email system privileges to send messages to discourage me, scare me, and / or offer me benefits or advice through emails. As this pattern has been uncovered before (where I protested and other students had protested that emails were being deleted, manipulated, and other tactics), the shocking factor is that all these emails attempt to further deceive, discourage, and offer me further benefits where my interest for particular area of the law was derived from subscriptions to ABA material and so forth.

VII. CONCLUSION

It is my hope that social justice can be found-where such deliberate, deceitful, and substantial steps were taken by this group of individuals under this sphere of influence. A group of individuals that work together through whatever means to stifle diversity and the minorities voice compromises the very sanctity of our democratic system.

A private professional education system funded by the Federal Government claiming to represent the diverse, the minority, where it would selectively manipulate and control by 'weeding' out those would did not conform is an attack on solidarity amongst others things.

Action must be taken and the truth must be heard. Otherwise these words stand for nothing, nay, we stand for nothing.

In conclusion, I have carefully preserved all the evidence that I have gathered where these words are merely a narrative and an explanation of these events. It is also my belief that upon further investigation, discovery, and other depositions- students will come forward with their stories and evidence where they were afraid and/or could not.

www.ingramcontent.com/pod-product-compliance
Lightning Source LLC
Chambersburg PA
CBHW030019190526
45157CB00016B/3163